AF498875

Group of International Communists

From each according to his ability,
to each according to his needs!

Group of International Communists
From each according to his ability,
to each according to his needs!
2021 Hermann Lueer (Editor/Translator)
herluee@yahoo.com
Red & Black Books
Bordesholmer Straße 22
22143 Hamburg, Germany
Cover: Niki Bong
mail@bongolai.de
ISBN 978-3-9822065-7-8

"There is no point in discussing "federalism or centralism" if you don't first show what the economic basis of this "federalism" or this "centralism" will be. In reality, the forms of organization of a given economy are not, on the whole, arbitrary forms, they are derived from the principles of that economy itself.

Therefore, it is insufficient to present the economy of communism only as a negation of the capitalist system: no money, no market, no private or state property. It is necessary to present its positive characters, to show what the economic laws will be, that will triumph over those of capitalism. If one proceeds in this way, it is very likely that the alternative "federalism or centralism" appears to be the wrong question."

Henk Canne Meijer

Foreword by the editor

"From each according to his ability, to each according to his needs!"[1]

This certainly most famous quotation of Karl Marx became the epitome of the communist society, in which Marxists and anarchists can unite until today. At the same time, the greatest misunderstanding, or rather the most fundamental revision of Marx's critique of political economy, is connected with this guiding principle.

Marx never distinguished between a socialist transitional phase and communism. For Marx, communism was realized with the successful social revolution, with the abolition of exploitative relations. Marx showed with his analysis of the economic relations that wherever one part of society owns the monopoly of the means of production, the worker, free or unfree, must provide a portion of his labor time to produce luxuries for the owner of the means of production. Only the form in which this additional labor is extorted from the immediate producer distinguishes the economic formations of society.[2]

As simple as the basis of the domination of the working class is, as simple was for Marx the derivation of the abolition of capitalist wage labor. This abolition can only

---

[1] Karl Marx, Critique of the Gotha Programme, Part I.
[2] Karl Marx, Capital, Volume I, p. 164 / 153

happen if the separation between worker and labor product is abolished if the right of disposal over the product of labor and thus over the means of production again belongs to the workers. In the association of free people, in which work with the means of production is done in common, in which the labor power of all the different individuals is consciously applied as the combined labor power of the community, the communally exercised disposition of the results of production by the free producers is the essential determination of communist society.[3]

For this, contrary to the opinion of most of the Marxists who refer to Marx, there is no need for a long and complicated path under the leadership of the party to reach, as Lenin put it, even the lowest stage of communism. On the contrary, "state communism" lacks from the outset the economic foundation on which to realize its ideal of the withering away of the state. With the nationalization of the means of production in the name of the people, wage labor is not abolished. Socialization of the means of production which does not at the same time abolish the separation between worker and labor product misses the goal since it maintains the exploitative relationship associated with wage labor. It lacks the fundamental economic basis of communist society, which enables the members of society to determine for themselves their working time and consumption – that is,

------

[3] Karl Marx, Capital, Volume I, p. 51,

what they want to have and how they want to work according to their individual weighing of effort and return.

Marx and Engels were not idealistic utopians who imagined a better world beyond the economic preconditions. They knew that the realm of freedom begins only where the work determined by necessity and external expediency ends; it lies, therefore, by its very nature beyond the sphere of actual material production. For Marx and Engels, however, communism was also not a project on the distant horizon of human history, when the productive forces have developed to such an extent that the realm of necessity has largely been overcome. For them, therefore rules on which all social labor must be based were indispensable for the planning of communist production following the social revolution. People cannot live in a community based on the division of labor and be free from it at the same time. Free producers, therefore, "cannot arbitrarily dispose of the means of production as do the "free producers" under capitalism (the factory owners or leaders). If the disposition is arbitrary, then there can be no question of communal disposition."[4]

Fifty years before Ludwig von Mieses had to enlighten the majority of Marxists that the abolition of the money measure without replacement is tantamount to the abolition of rationality in the economy, Marx and Engels al-

---

[4] Group of International Communists, Fundamental Principles of Communist Production and Distribution, Red & Black Books 2020, p 25

ready knew that with the help of the labor-time calculation the individual desire to consume and the individual willingness to work can be brought into the social planning process. "The useful effects of the various articles of consumption, compared with one another and with the quantities of labor required for their production, will, in the end, determine the plan. People will be able to manage everything very simply, without the intervention of much-vaunted 'value'."[5] Only on this basis can the *collectively* exercised disposition of the means of production by the *free* producers be transformed from phrase to reality. That is, everyone can determine his own working time and consumption. In terms of content, the working time calculation is nothing other than the factual reconciliation of the division of labor carried out in the common planning.

With the labor-time calculation the bourgeois legal horizon – *in principle* – is inevitably connected, since "the right of the producers is *proportional* to the labor they supply; the equality consists in the fact that measurement is made with an *equal standard*, labor."[6] This bothers many Marxists and anarchists, like holy water does the devil. However, the intellectual-philosophical dispute as to whether the labor-time calculation is *only a transitional form to complete community and free use of social resources,* and thus whether the narrow bourgeois legal horizon can be completely transcended, is not relevant to the decision

---

[5] F. Engels, Anti-Dühring, Part III: Socialism, IV. Distribution
[6] Karl Marx, Critique of the Gotha Programme, Part I.

of the majority of people. Based on the labor time calculation, the majority of the world population would have already won in comparison to the capitalist production relations, despite the *"inevitable bourgeois legal horizon"*. The same right is here still – *in principle* – the bourgeois right, but with fundamentally different content. The regulation of production and consumption through the calculation of working time no longer permits class distinctions, and whether individual labor is socially recognized is no longer determined behind the backs of the members of society in the competition on the market but is already determined with the common planning.

After the productive forces have increased with the all-around development of the individual, and all the springs of co-operative wealth flow more abundantly, *after* the enslaving subordination of the individual to the division of labor, and therewith also the antithesis between mental and physical labor has vanished, *after* labor has become not only a means of life but life's prime want, *only then* – when the realm of necessity has been overcome – the narrow bourgeois legal horizon can be completely transcended and everyone can simply do what he wants.

> "Any distribution whatever of the means of consumption is only a consequence of the distribution of the conditions of production themselves. The latter distribution, however, is a feature of the mode of production itself. … Vulgar socialism has taken over from the bourgeois economists the consideration and treatment

of distribution as independent of the mode of production and hence the presentation of socialism as turning principally on distribution. After the real relation has long been made clear, why retrogress again?"[7]

The fundamental principles of communist production and distribution derived from Marx and Engels' Critique of Political Economy were already presented in detail in 1930 by the Group of International Communists under the corresponding title. In addition, numerous articles were published by members of the group from the mid-1920s to the end of the 1930s, which have lost none of their topicality to this day. They provide a fundamental critique of the various currents based on Marxism, anarchism or, more generally, socialism – all to encourage workers to "take over the management and administration of production and distribution themselves, in accordance with generally adopted social rules to realize the *Association of Free and Equal Producers*. The GIC sees the essential progress of the workers' movement in the development of workers' self-consciousness. Therefore, it confronts the leadership politics of the parliamentary parties and the trade union movement with the slogan:

All power to the workers' councils.

Production in the hands of the enterprise organizations."[8]

---

[7] Karl Marx, Critique of the Gotha Programme, Part I.
[8] GIC, Fundamental Principles, p. 5

Workers' Councils and Communist Organization of Economy [9]

Wage labor and the state economy

Because private ownership of the means of production stands in the way of a rational economy, indeed, in the permanent crisis prevents the application of the productive forces at all, the abolition of private ownership appears as the next goal. From this follows the consolidation of the economy under the central power of the state. And here it is the task of scientists, statisticians, engineers, etc., to carry out the actual construction. Thus, the socialist economic organization appears as an organizational problem, as an absolute generalization and completion of the tendency already preformed by capitalism in the formation of trusts and cartels. The state becomes a mammoth trust which, through organization, overcomes the obstacles standing in the way of further development of production. The socialism that

---

[9] First published in: Internationale Rätekorrespondenz (International Council Correspondence) Nr. 5 *October 1934*. Theoretical and Discussion Organ for the Councils Movement. Issue of the Group of International Communists - Holland.
Translation: Hermann Lueer
The original text has been shortened in some places for this edition, and the extensive footnotes with references to Lenin quotations have been omitted, since they are cited in a similar form in the following article "Marx-Engels and Lenin".

one wants to build, therefore, turns out to be a state economy which — with planned management of the economy, with the elimination of destructive competition and capital profit, and with the full application of the increased productive forces — intends to raise the living conditions of the masses in general.

Russian development has proved that such a state economy can be nothing other than state capitalism. The worker remains a wage laborer, now bound by the state's obligation to work. He works in state enterprises and sells his labor power to the state. His wage is the price the state pays him for it. Thus, the state takes the place of the expropriated private capitalist. It is the state which now exercises command over wage labor and thus also dominates and exploits the workers.

Labor power, just as in private capitalism, becomes a commodity: it is equated with a product already produced (the means of subsistence that the worker receives through the wage). It becomes a commodity, which also means that it is degraded to a thing, stripped of all personal will. It is transformed from subject to object. But since the worker cannot be separated from his labor-power, the same is true for the wage-laborer, he is degraded to a thing, to an object, used by the owner of the means of production as "a means to produce". There is no need for further discussion to be able to say that with the fact that in this state economy, announced as socialism, the worker remains a wage laborer, his social position is also decided.

But the Russian example not only shows that the announced socialism is in fact state capitalism. Not only has it been proven that state production is not production for needs, but ordinary commodity production. There also emerged a new ruling stratum that disposes of state property and thus occupies a privileged position. This stratum is interested in the further expansion of state power because it is precisely this state power that guarantees its privileged position in society. It also gives the direction in the further development, because in its hands are concentrated all material means and other forces of the society. And what can it do but strive for the increase of the state property and enlargement of the state power? Once social production is shaped as state management, it follows a development determined by the power relations it creates.

The workers are expropriated, every day anew, when they perform work; and this by the state, the sole owner, who appropriates the products of labor. The state is the owner, the administrator of the social wealth. He is the organizer, leader, and director of the social production process. And he is at the same time the power that determines the level of individual consumption and the allocation of goods. He is a social organization that is best understood if one thinks of the administrative apparatus of all private capitalist enterprises, joint-stock companies, united with the political power of the state. The state as the sole manager is nothing other than such an amalgamation of all the administrative organs of private property: for just as the administration of private capital is unproductive and serves only as an organ for the appropriation of the fruits of other people's labor, so also the bureaucratic apparatus of the state creates no product and has no other task than to secure for the state what is produced by wage labor in the state enterprises.

The development of state management is thus characterized by a dichotomy that must continually deepen. On the one hand, accumulation of property and power in the hands of the state bureaucracy, for *it* is the state; on the other, the wage laborers whose labor products are appropriated by the state.

The more the wealth of society as state property grows, the greater the exploitation of wage laborers, the more powerless they are. As the wealth of society as state property grows, so does the misery of the wage-workers; the class struggle between wage-workers and the state bureaucracy is its necessary consequence. To assert itself in this struggle, the bureaucracy has no choice but to expand the repressive apparatus of the state; it must grow in the same measure as the rift deepens, the richer the state, the greater the misery of the workers, the sharper the class struggle.

The Proletarian problem

The wage workers cannot be satisfied with this "socialism", even if it should bless them with material goods (which, by the way, is very doubtful). They must strive to have the rule of capital abolished for them as well.

Their struggle is directed toward abolishing the capital relation itself; that they no longer be bought as labor power and placed in the production process as a productive force, equal to the machines, under the command of the new rulers. They must themselves become the masters of production, of their own and the mechanical productive forces. They themselves must take possession of the means of production to manage and administer them in the name of society, under responsibility to that society. They themselves must rise to become the leader and manager of production, the administrator and distributor of the goods produced if they wish to unite humanity in the classless society and not fall again into servitude themselves.

From this striving, differently than with the intellectuals, also another problem arises, new points of view open. It gives rise to conceptions of the regulation of the mutual relations of men in social production which seem incomprehensible to the intellectual elite and which they declare utopian and impracticable. But these conceptions have already developed a tremendous force in the revolutionary uprisings of the wage workers, the modern proletarians. This force first showed itself on a larger scale in the Paris Commune, which sought to overcome the central power of the state through the self-government of the communes. It also caused, among other things, Marx to abandon his view that the state economy would bring about the overcoming of class society (laid down in the "Communist Manifesto"). In the Workers' and Soldiers' Councils of the Russian and German revolutions of 1917-23, it rose anew to enormous, at times all-dominating power. And in the future, no proletarian revolutionary movement is conceivable in which it will not play an ever more prominent, finally all-dominating role. It is the self-action of the broad working masses that manifests itself in the workers' councils. Here there is nothing utopian anymore, it is a real reality. In the workers' councils, the proletariat has created the organizational form in which it leads its liberation struggle.

Thus, it is then no utopia, no empty theory, that these workers' councils, where they are grouped around production, in the workplaces, as operational organizations, want to take possession of the means of production themselves and to direct and manage production themselves. It is a demand that will be raised by broad masses of workers in the course of development. And the intellectual stratum will have to suppress this aspiration by force if it wants to assert its command in the state economy.

From the point of view of the workers' councils, the problem in the questions of economic organization is not how production must be mastered and best organized, but how the mutual relations of men to each other and among themselves are to be regulated in connection with the production. For production, in their eyes, is no longer an objective process in which man's labor and the product of it are separated from him, a process which one computes and directs like lifeless material, but to them, production is the vital function of the workers themselves. If production - the expression of man's life when everyone has to work - is already socially in practice, then man's participation in it, his own expression of life, can also be socially regulated, without in turn equating them with their own instruments of labor and subjecting them to the command of a special stratum. Once the problem is posed in this way, then the resolution is also not so improbable and quite easy to find. It offers itself here, too, as if by itself. It is the work of men themselves, their own expression of life in the field of production, which serves as the standard for the regulation of relations among themselves. Once the labor of individuals, as well as their association in operational organizations, has been introduced as the determining factor in the social regulation of the mutual relations, there is no longer a place for any management and leadership that do not participate in production themselves, that only exercise functions of domination and appropriate the products of others.

The Workers' Councils

No leader of Social Democracy, not even Lenin, had recognized the importance of workers' councils before 1917, and yet they already played an important role in the Russian Revolution of 1905 in Petersburg. Only when in 1917 in Russia, then in Germany, etc., the workers' councils proved to be the form of struggle of the revolutionary proletariat, when the broad masses of workers decisively influenced politics and the economy through the workers' councils, only then did the attention of the political greats of Social Democracy turn to them. But not at all in the sense of perceiving in them the first, independent step of the proletariat in the direction of taking its fate in its own hands. The workers' councils are for them a new manifestation of that force that must serve to bring them to power themselves. In their eyes, the proletariat, this enormous and still growing social force, is only a social force, as the forces of production in the factories - a force that is used to achieve certain results, to realize elaborated plans. Such is the thinking of the intellectual as leader of the capitalist production process, and such is also his thinking when, as a social democrat, he intends to lead the social forces. The proletariat has no independent thinking with him; it thinks and acts as its leaders think. That is why the "Revolutionary Marxist Party" ... must have the leadership in its hands if the proletarian forces are to be employed under the socialist plans. If it is not the Revolutionary Marxist, then it is just another party that needs the strength of the proletariat to carry out its particular plans and intentions. Whoever sees things from this point of view can come to no other conclusion than: *Without the leadership of the party, no socialism.*

From this point of view, the workers' councils appear as new organs of the proletariat in which leadership must be conquered; they must become the instrument in the hands of the leadership to influence the thought and action of the masses. ... But the force emanating from the workers' councils came about precisely in the opposite way. It was the will of the masses born in the workplaces and mass meetings, which raised deputies and delegates from the masses as spokesmen, ready at any moment to stand up for them with the utmost means. This will of the masses formed until now only in connection with a few quite general problems, the resolution of which, after all, nobody could prevent. Thus, the will of the masses in Russia in 1917 and Germany in 1918 was directed to the termination of the war. The war had to be ended, whatever the cost; all objections to it, artificial, acquired, and rooted in the masses themselves, were finally set aside. Consequently, everywhere the general will was formed to put an end to the war and to take up the struggle against the military power of one's own country for this purpose. The workers' and soldiers' councils were only the organizational forms in which this will was translated into action. Hence the workers' councils are only possible as an expression and organizational form of the will of broad masses of workers, whereby one must not lose sight of the fact that such a will is formed only under certain conditions and is certainly not brought about by the slogans of this or that party.

Now, when the "Revolutionary Marxist Party" strives for leadership in the workers' councils, it goes the opposite way. It wants to use these organs of mass will as a means to make the masses act according to the will and plans of the "leaders". The leader, however, can see the masses only as the material with which he must work, and in this, the independent will of the masses is a hostile element.

That is why the workers' councils under the leadership of a party are deprived of their own power, and if they live on, it is only by deception; that is, by concealing from the masses the fact that they have become instruments in the hands of the leaders. This was also the fate of the workers' councils in Russia and Germany, after the first goal, the ending of the war, had been achieved and opinions had diverged regarding the reorganization of the social order, - a unified will thus no longer existed among the working masses.

They were "conquered" by the competing party tendencies, soon lost their influence on the working masses, and therefore have no more value for the party policy of the leaders. They disappeared. Only in the plans of the "revolutionary Marxist" parties, which are preparing to conquer the leadership in the coming mass uprising, do they live on as organs through which one intends to lead the masses.

And yet, the spirit that was expressed in the revolutionary workers' councils is not dead. The essential thing is that in these organs the workers find the unification of their class forces, the overcoming of their division into unions, parties, tendencies. When the workers find this unity in the daily class struggle; when they lead the struggle themselves through spontaneously formed organs, setting aside the old organizations that separate them from one another, then the spirit of the revolutionary workers' councils is again in the working masses, then the masses reveal their will.

In today's struggles, we see again and again the beginnings of this class action, but we also see at the same time the attempts of the old workers' movement, which up to now have almost always succeeded, to wrest the leadership of the struggle away from the workers to transfer it to the trade union bureaus. Just as the "communist" economy of the leaders is to be carried out via the detour of the state bureaucracy, so also the leadership of the struggle is to be withdrawn from the direct power of disposal of the workers and diverted via the trade union apparatus.

But the power of the ruling class under capitalism is so immense that only the power of the whole undivided working class can overcome it.

Thus, class relations tell us that the workers can only win when they have overcome the old workers' movement through their council unity, that they can only win when the "legislative and executive power" in the struggles is exercised by the masses themselves.

All power to the workers' councils

But this slogan has meaning only if the power of the councils is the expression of the united will of broad working masses, indeed, of the whole working class.

Unity in the will and action of the whole working class is the soil on which the power of workers' councils grows. For this, it is not enough if broad masses in extreme need put an end to an intolerable state of affairs by their own action. This is how they acted in 1918 and only forced the end of the war. There must be added the positive will to transform society, to reorganize the relations of people in this society.

The one thing, the intolerable condition, is taken care of by capitalist society itself. The living situation of the working class is becoming more and more untenable; wage labor is becoming a curse for an ever-growing mass of millions, a horror from which it is impossible to escape. The situation finally comes to a head in such a way that in broad masses the will is born to end this untenable condition, no matter what the cost. But they cannot end it without abolishing wage labor at the same time. Even the state socialism of the leaders does not bring salvation, because it lets wage labor continue to exist, organized anew by the state power. Therefore, action under the constraint of extreme necessity must be accompanied by the conscious transformation of social conditions. The ending of the state of emergency and the reorganization of social relations are *one* act; they are only two sides of the same action. From the untenable condition for the masses of workers, who as wage-workers are exposed to absolute impoverishment, there is only this one salvation, that the wage-workers themselves take possession of the means of production. But they can only do this if they unite in the councils to become the social power and at the same time jointly, i.e. on a communist basis, use the means of production for social needs.

Communist economy

The council's power abolishes wage labor, it makes the worker the determining factor in production. Its task is to realize the liberation of the working class by making wage laborers free and equal producers. But these free and equal producers must regulate their relations with each other. The firm regulation of these relations, by which the equality and consequently the freedom of the producers is guaranteed, becomes the all-dominant law, which is finally the bold foundation on which communist society rests.

But this regulation is nothing else than the regulation of the metabolic process in society, - the regulation of production and consumption, of the participation of the individual producer in the production of goods and his consumption of the jointly produced goods. And, where the work of the individual producer is at the same time his participation in the common production of goods, it can be nothing else than that this work also decides on his share in the produced goods. Labor, measured by the time of its activity, the labor hour, must, as a social measure, regulate the relations of producers among themselves. The individual, special labor hour of the individual producer, however, is not a social measure; it is different in each case and always anew. Therefore, the social-average working hour, the average of all the different working hours, must be found and raised to the status of a social-regulating factor.

It is impossible here to describe in more detail the movement of communist economic life based on the social-average working hour. For this, read: "Fundamental Principles of Communist Production and Distribution" – edition of the G.I.C. We limit ourselves to pointing out the implementation of the labor-time calculation in the communist economy as a direct goal, and thus do not consider it as something that "will be found later".

The economic promotion of the labor-time account expresses itself politically in the domination of society by the workers. One is not without the other. If the working class is incapable of carrying out the labor-time calculation, it means nothing else than that it is incapable of abolishing wage labor; incapable of usurping the direction and administration of social life. If working time does not become the measure of individual consumption, then wage labor is the only solution. That is, there is then no direct relationship between producers and social wealth. It means that through wage labor the separation of the worker from the social product has become a fact. Or the same thing said in other words: the management of the production process cannot be in the hands of the workers. The management of the production process passes over to the "statisticians" and other scientists who are charged with the distribution of the "national income". Either abolition of wage labor, with the social-average hour of labor as the fulcrum of the whole economy, under self-management of all workers, or wage labor in the service of the state.

Therefore, we raise as a direct slogan of workers' power: The workers bring all social functions under their direct administration. They appoint and remove all functionaries. The workers take the social production into their own management by uniting in operational organizations and workers' councils. They themselves switch their operations to the communist economy by calculating their production according to the average social working time. Thus, the whole society goes over to communist production. Thus, there are not operational units that are "ripe" for social management and operational units that are not yet "ripe".

This is the political and at the same time economic program of the wage workers; in this sense, their councils will transform the economy. These are the highest demands we can make in these questions, but at the same time, they are also the lowest, because it is a question of the being or not being of the proletarian revolution.

What must be done? [10]

The collapse of the old workers' movement is organizationally and ideologically final and can no longer be stopped. In general, therefore, there is a widespread feeling of powerlessness, and out of this desperate situation all groups and little groups are whining about fragmentation, and all want somehow to establish the united front of the proletariat. Some believe that this can be done with powerful united front guards, but only under their leadership, others with unions, fusions, and other artificial, even artful combinations. All these efforts are attempts on an unsuitable object and are doomed to failure from the outset. This result is the necessary consequence of the already mentioned fundamentally wrong attitude, because one sees all processes purely mechanically and not as a process, as a development. Yes, because one has no idea at all of the real problems that

---

[10] First published in: Internationale Rätekorrespondenz (International Council Correspondence) Nr. 16/17 *Mai 1936*. Theoretical and Discussion Organ for the Councils Movement. Issue of the Group of International Communists - Holland.
Translation: Hermann Lueer
First English translation published in: International Council Correspondence, Vol. II (1935-1936), No 12 (November 1936)
http://www.aaap.be/Pdf/International-Council-Correspondence/International-Council-Correspondence-2-12a.pdf

stand before the workers' movement. In decades of work, one has put together a wishful building of the character of the workers' revolution, which of course had to collapse at the first serious onslaught of the class opponents. It would be understandable now to have an objective investigation of the shameful collapse, but instead of that one muddles merrily on in the old rut, as if nothing had happened. ...

To take things as they really are means: to bring the revolutionary interest to bear in a form corresponding to and adapted to the changed circumstances.

And this is what matters!

Fact is: Everything old is past, never to return - things must start anew. This orientation is above all an ideological, spiritual starting from the beginning. The ideological foundations of the old workers' movement have collapsed. And not only nationally, but also internationally. The German situation is a prime example of the international development. The political development to fascist methods of government and economically to state capitalism proves: For the social transformation of society, it is not enough to make only a change in the political superstructure, to put a better government in place of the old one. To have a fascist government instead of a bourgeois-liberal one, a Bolshevik government instead of a socialist one. Such a transformation changes the external face of society but leaves its internal structure essentially untouched. The Soviet Russian example shows:

Even a Socialist-Bolshevik government retains the wage system. The intention is probably to make a better distribution of national income by paying higher socialist wages. But as long as wage labor prevails, capitalism exists. Wage labor and capital are two sides of the same thing. Wage labor presupposes capital, capital presupposes wage labor. One is not possible without the other. Marx proved this more than 60 years ago. Thus, we see as a result of the old workers' movement that its struggle leads to a revolution from above, where a change of government is made under the socialist flag, but the masses are excluded from determining the character of the new society, and economically wage labor continues to be maintained as the economic basis. Thus, however, all the preconditions of capitalism are preserved. The abolition of private property of the means of production alone has nothing to do with communism, as Marx has also already demonstrated.

Now, if the road to a classless society is really to be taken, one of the most essential conditions is that the masses *themselves* decisively influence the development of the revolution of the new society and act as its sole carrier. The self-liberation of the proletariat presupposes that all matters are tackled by them alone. They must do everything alone, no one can take the struggle for the social reorganization of society from them. Let us not be under any illusions: The time of surprise revolutions carried out by small, conscious minorities at the head of unconscious masses is over. Where it is a question of a complete transformation of the social organization, the masses *themselves must be involved,* must themselves have already understood what it is about, what they are to stand up for. And that is what matters. *The masses, by exercising power, must learn to exercise power!* There is no other way to teach it this. The self-action of the masses through their own organs - councils, responsible only to themselves and eliminating any clique of leaders and organizations - is the precondition of the social revolution. All other ways lead back to the bourgeois revolution and capitalism, no matter how revolutionary they are draped.

For this struggle of the workers to lead to a complete transformation of society and a new economic form – and this is the real character of the proletarian revolution – there must be clarity about the preconditions of the new economic form. The focus must be on the immediate abolition of wage labor in every form and the establishment of a correct relationship of producers to the product and the means of production. *It is these two tasks that constitute the content of the social revolution.* With the abolition of wage labor and the monetary calculation, the exploitation of man by man is abolished. But so that exploitation may be abolished forever, the right of disposal over social development in every form must rest with the producers, and no operational or statistical bureaucracy may be allowed to develop which, by the detour of the "just distribution of products," may arrive at a new domination of the producers.

From capitalist to communist mode of production!

The foundation of capitalism is wage slavery. The precondition of wage labor is the separation of the producers from the means of production, the condemnation of the workers to lifelong wage slavery. The exploitation of human beings, the production of surplus-value (profit), and thus also the economic crisis mechanisms are based on wage slavery. Because in the capitalist mode of production, *"the products now produced socially were not appropriated by those who had actually set in motion the means of production and actually produced the commodities, but by the capitalists. The means of production, and production itself, had become in essence socialized. But they were subjected to a form of appropriation which presupposes the private production of individuals, under which, therefore, everyone owns his own product and brings it to market. The mode of production is subjected to this form of appropriation, although it abolishes the conditions upon which the latter rests. This contradiction, which gives to the new mode of production its capitalistic character, contains the germ of the whole of the social antagonisms of today."*[11]

The capitalist wage system is thus the basic contradiction of the profit order, from which the economic crises and catastrophes spring.

The tremendous development of the productive forces, the unlimited expansion of production, the international triumph of the capitalist regime through the creation of

---

[11] Frederick Engels, Socialism: Utopian and Scientific. III [Historical Materialism]

the world market, the violent concentration of capital in joint-stock companies and trusts, – all these revolutionary economic processes have increased the contradictions of capitalism to the point of absurdity, which is erupting in the prevailing world crisis. The international crisis of the profit system, on the one hand, throws the working masses to a level of barbarism, on the other hand, it is the driving force of a state-capitalist transformation of the bourgeois social order. Through state economic planning, the life of capital, the production of surplus value, is to be secured. The interventions of the state in the production process (to a planned control) probably limit the economic power of the bourgeoisie, – but through the state-capitalist transformation, nothing is changed in principle in the capitalist mode of production. Even the general nationalization (as it is carried out in Soviet Russia) does not mean the abolition of the capital property of the means of production, as well as the elimination of the commodity character of the products and the human labor power. For in state capitalism, too, there is the domination of accumulated labor over living labor, that is, the domination of the product over the producers, and thus the relation of exploitation. The only difference is that the superfluous bourgeois class is replaced by the state itself as the only giant trust of exploitation. *The economic programs of Social Democracy and Bolshevism (as explained elsewhere) are all based on a state economy. They are therefore essentially related to the capitalist mode of pro-*

duction since they mean only a continuation of wage slavery. Communism alone is the lever for the economic liberation of the proletariat.

So, what are the basic lines of the communist mode of production?

At the center of the proletarian revolution is the overthrow of capitalism, that is, the abolition of the wage system. This goal can, of course, only be achieved through a political struggle for power, which, however, must not lead to a new form of state-socialist domination of the working classes. It is therefore the core question in the (social) revolution to create a direct fundamental relationship of the producer to the social product, which makes the formation of a new apparatus of oppression impossible. Karl Max, in his socio-scientific research work, especially based on the experience of the Paris Commune, concluded that the organization of the communist economy can only come about through an association (union) of free and equal producers. The association has nothing to do with the idealistic world improvement plans of the socialist utopians floating in the air but has a very material basis. The firm basis is the socially average labor time, that is, the calculation of the time needed to produce the products. Marx and Engels clearly enough referred to the labor hour as the unit of calculation for the production process.

"Society can simply calculate how many hours of labor go into a steam engine, a hectoliter of wheat from the last harvest, and so on. But it cannot occur to it to express the quanta of labor laid down in the products, which it then knows absolutely and directly, still further in a third product, instead of in their natural, appropriate absolute measure of time."[12]

The same applies to consumption. Marx remarks on this in Capital, Vol. I, among other things:

"Labor-time serves as a measure of the portion of the common labor borne by each individual, and of his share in the part of the total product destined for individual consumption. The social relations of the individual producers, with regard both to their labor and to its products, are in this case perfectly simple and intelligible, and that with regard not only to production but also to distribution. "[13]

By elevating the labor-time account to the general standard for production and distribution, Marx and Engels laid the foundation for an exact relationship between producer and product. The social-legal determination of this basic relationship is the unconditional prerequisite for the fact that the right of disposal over production is connected with productive labor. Only socialization of the means of production on this revolutionary basis leads to the elimination of the capitalist commodity economy and thus to the overthrow of the rule of the product over the producer. But where this direct relation

---

[12] F. Engels, Anti-Dühring, part III socialism, IV Distribution
[13] Karl Marx, Capital vol. 1, p. 51

of the producer to the product is not established, a new form of exploitation must inevitably develop. The Soviet Union offers an instructive example in this respect. Through nationalization, the Russian proletariat is only ostensibly the owner of the means of production, for the power of disposal over production lies with the "Supreme People's Economic Council." The Bolshevik central leadership determines what share the producer receives from the social stock of products. It is not the producers who, with their work, at the same time determine their share of the product according to the labor-time calculation, but this share is determined by the experts of the state economic management through "price policy". This personal decision on the distribution of the product has as a consequence the continuation of the old struggle for positions of power because the central economic power is at the same time political power. And whoever possesses the state power also possesses the total social product and controls the distribution of the same. Thus the old opposition between society and state, between producers and government, continues. The producer is dependent on the ruling bureaucracy, which assigns him the product based on "expert statistics"; he is a wage laborer! The Bolshevik state socialism in Soviet Russia has thus a production apparatus which rises above the producers and dominates them, i.e. despite the abolition of the private property of the means of production the system of exploitation continues in another form! The contrast between "state socialism" and association is thus in reality the contrast between capitalism and communism.

In contrast, in the communist association, there is no longer any place for a special apparatus of power over the producer. Here it is not the state which has the direction and administration of production and distribution, but these functions are exercised by the producers and consumers. Whereas the reformist theory of socialization or nationalization of the "already mature enterprises" means in practice only a continuation of capitalist concentration, in Marxian socialization the economy as a whole is ripe for communism. What matters is precise that the revolutionary initiative is unleashed in all the enterprises so that the proletarians themselves can build the edifice of the communist mode of production. *This construction is a process from below, which can only be carried out by the producers, and no decree from above can replace this revolutionary economic practice of the masses.* By introducing the labor-time account as the general basis of the production process, economic power passes into the hands of the working class. Because the relation of the producers to the social product now lies in the things themselves, and the individual share in the product is determined solely by the material production itself and directly. The entire process of production thus stands on real ground, because it is precisely in this basic relationship that the masses can direct and regulate the course of the economy themselves. Thus, also the justification for the existence of a bureaucratic apparatus, which controls the distribution by "price policy", is irrevocably abolished. In other words, the conditions for the death of the state are now in place, since the intervention of state organs of power in economic relations has become superfluous. That social order has been reached which Engels characterizes with the sentences:

> "The society which reorganizes production through the association of free and equal producers replaces the whole state machine where it will then belong: in the museum of antiquities, next to the spinning wheel and the bronze ax. … The government of persons is replaced by the administration of things and the management of production processes. The state is not 'abolished', it dies."[14]

In communism, the *distribution of consumer goods is a social function* that takes place collectively. Therefore, the association of producers implies the association of free and equal consumers in the form of consumer cooperatives. The communist economic order knows only the equal distribution of the social product among all consumers, whereby labor power ceased to be a commodity. The elimination of any "price policy" also makes the capitalist market superfluous, since the needs of the masses are collectively expressed in the distribution organizations

---

[14] Frederick Engels, Origin of the Family, Private Property, and the State, p. 94 / Frederick Engels, Socialism: Utopian and Scientific

to be created. Likewise, communism means the abolition of money, which is replaced by the calculation of working time. With the help of key figures (index figures) the conversion to the new unit of value is carried out. Marx already writes about the abolition of the capitalist money calculation in Capital, Vol. III:

> "Money capital falls away in social production. Society distributes means of production and labor power into the various branches of business. The producers may receive paper instructions, for which they withdraw from the social stocks of consumption a quantum corresponding to their labor time. These instructions are not money. They do not circulate."[15]

The introduction of labor money is therefore not a utopia, but a real necessity of the communist mode of production.

Of course, the distribution of consumer goods itself has as a prerequisite that the producer cannot receive the "full yield" of his labor. Because the production process consumes in its perpetual flow not only human labor but also machines, raw materials, auxiliary materials, etc., which must also be renewed to enable production to continue. In addition, society must maintain a group of "unproductive" plants or public enterprises, as well as cultural facilities, whose energy consumption must likewise be borne by the entire economic process. Thus, as

---

[15] Karl Marx, Capital Vol.2, chapter 18, 2. The role of money-capital

Marx notes in his "Critique of the Gotha Program", the following must be deducted from the total social product: cover for the replacement of the means of production consumed, an additional part for the expansion of production, and a reserve fund against accidents, disturbances caused by natural events, etc. Before it comes to the individual division of the total product remaining as means of consumption, there are again deducted from it: funds for the school, health care, etcetera, funds for the incapable of work, and finally a part for general administration, which, however, is considerably restricted in comparison with the bourgeois system and sinks to a minimum. Thus, only the shortened labor contract can be distributed among the consumers, since the deductions are an economic necessity. The amount of social accumulation, however, must always be determined by the producers, so that no administrative apparatus can arbitrarily determine the amount of accumulation based on statistical surveys, since in any case the disproportion then arising between social accumulation and the capacity to consume would soon restore the capitalist trouble spot. Reproduction and accumulation are, on a communist basis, social functions that the proletariat can precisely control through its general accounting (i.e., the labor-time account) and, moreover, has the right of disposal over the use of the funds. This social accounting is very simple and can be carried out at any time by any worker who knows how to read and write. Therefore, no specialists of any kind are needed for this. …

These are the essential fundamental lines of the communist mode of production. They apply not only to industry but also to agriculture. This is because, as a result of capitalist development, the peasants have fallen into the same dependency as the proletariat. They are forced by the socialization of production to integrate themselves into the new economic order. The economic dictatorship of the communist association discards any right of exploitation and excludes from its community anyone who does not recognize this principle. But by taking the management of production into their own hands through their operational organizations and councils, the producers at the same time lay the foundation for a development in which the dictatorship eventually becomes superfluous and abolishes itself. *Based on association, the proletarian dictatorship is only a transitional stage to a classless society.* By introducing a socially planned regulation of production according to the collective needs of the totality, communism replaces the capitalist mode of appropriation by the mode of appropriation of products founded in the very nature of the modern means of production: on the one hand, direct social appropriation as a means of maintaining and expanding production; on the other hand, direct individual appropriation as a means of life and enjoyment. Thus, the antisocial struggle for individual existence ceases and the division of society into an exploiting and an exploited, into a ruling and an oppressed class disappears. *Thus, the association of the free and equal producers - to channel Engels - is nothing else than the leap of mankind from the realm of necessity into the realm of freedom!*

43

Leninism is State Capitalism[16]

One must be struck with blindness not to recognize that in the economic teachings of Bolshevism, in its conception of the organization of the national economy and the economic policy arising from it, there lies a straight line which in the result finally leads to that new type of system of exploitation which we call state capitalism.

Already in 1917, *Lenin* outlined the basic lines of this new economic organization in his writing "The State and Revolution", and the policy of the Bolsheviks to this day is a unique continuation of the path once taken, which naturally acquires its specific practical face in the flow of life. Lenin demands as the task of the dictatorship of the proletariat *the organization of the whole economy "according to the pattern of a state capitalist trust."* All the measures of the Russian government are clearly aimed at the implementation of this principle. It has already been carried out in the state-managed industry. Central trading companies in the field of circulation and productive cooperatives in the cities and the countryside are to bring the remaining part of the economy under state control. "Consolidation into a trust" is the guiding principle of state economic policy in Russia. And the dispute as to whether the

---

[16] Second part of an article by Max Hempel (pseudonym of Jan Appel), Das russische Wiederaufbauprogramm (The Russian Reconstruction Program), from: Proletarier, *1926*, Vol. 10, p. 175. Translation: Hermann Lueer

state's undertakings can be addressed as socialist is only about whether to call such state trust "socialism."

However, when put into practice, it becomes clear that the state can only summarize and manage the economy as it is, i.e. an economy which is to a large extent directly private, which - because the balance of goods cannot be achieved by state bureaucratic means - requires a free market and which, in the absence of any other economic regulation, is based on the exploitation of "free" wage labor.

"State socialism" is wage slavery

As far as the *private* economy exists and will remain in this system, the surplus product of the exploited labor power comes into the hands of the private users of the foreign labor power. The surplus product of the workers in the state enterprises is at the disposal of the state itself, which is not a chimerical idea here either, but receives the real face of the bureaucracy possessing and exercising power. Stalin has given us telling examples of how the bureaucracy manages with it.

The economic concerns of the state can now be no other than those of the private capitalists. They press above all for greater productivity of labor, try to improve the organization of the economy, and cheapen the administrative apparatus. This is nothing other than what the corporations and trusts in capitalist countries also carry out: Rationalization of the economy. Assuming that the Russian state succeeds in the rationalization wrapped in socialist phrases by the Bolsheviks, the possible result remains precisely only a strengthening of the state economy. The larger scale of the state economy brings a larger mass of surplus product or surplus-value, which are at the disposal of the state and serve for this purpose - for further socialist accumulation. Where is the end here or in other words: How is the interest of the producer, the wage-worker, preserved in this development? The Bolsheviks are never at a loss for an answer and refer, for example, to the reports of the workers' delegations to Russia, which above all knew how to tell of rest homes and other social benefits from the state. However, they deliberately overlook the fact that it is primarily the state bureaucracy that provides for itself and its servants in this way, and that a social gradation necessarily prevails in this area as well. *A unique "socialism", by the way, which first exploits the workers to give them state social benefits later.*

Russian workers are also promised wage increases by the state as a result of higher productivity. Although in practice one sees nothing of this - when wages are nominally increased, prices also rise, as in any other country - even if there is, in fact, an increase in the living standards of workers, this is by no means something peculiar to socialism. American industry has raised labor productivity to the maximum and gives workers far higher wages than capitalism in Europe. On the other hand, in Russia it is the state, i.e. the bureaucracy that embodies it, that determines whether and to what extent wages are to be raised and how social benefits are to be paid in general. The state of workers and peasants - the short formula for the economic doctrine of Leninism - is the guarantee of socialism. Accordingly, the whole economic policy of the Bolsheviks is directed toward the nationalization of the economy and is in full harmony with the actual course of development in Russia.

State faith and leader power

According to Leninism, all life is concentrated in the state, all the energies of society flow to it as the central culmination point, and from it, in turn, the unified energy radiates back to all the members of society. Thus, this doctrine must become a complicated mechanical system of social life into which the multiform flow of things is tried to be squeezed. With necessity, the question of the implementation of communism, that is, of the right of disposal of the producers expropriated by capital over the recaptured means of production, is thereby shifted to the field where the workers must struggle for a greater or lesser influence on the mechanical, bureaucratic administrative apparatus. Opportunities for this are provided by Soviet elections, activity in the trade unions, and the ruling party. Through these channels, the will of the workers and peasants is to be directed to the central government power, which then radiates out from here via the supreme national economic council, the trust lines, and other central administrative bodies, finally meeting the workers again in the person of the "red director". One does not even need to be an ABC-scholar of Marxism to know what transformation the "will of the people" undergoes in this way.

The fact of *domination* and *exploitation* is not altered by any system, however sophisticated, that seeks to let the workers and peasants determine *state policy*; it exists and is exercised through the bureaucratic state apparatus. The only way to make progress *within this system* is to "democratize" the state.

The emerging state economic colossus in Russia, which presents itself with all repugnance even in its youth, is not only the result of special Russian conditions but at the same time also the product of the active intervention of the Bolsheviks, who in this context embody a very specific school of thought of the old workers' movement. A common thread running through social democracy from Lasalle to Lenin is the belief in the omnipotence of the state. The views vary in detail, but they converge at the focal point where the state, that is, the centralized political power of command with the aid of production – as with Lassalle – or through dictatorship - as with Lenin – solves the social problem. Behind the cult of the state, there is in reality disbelief in the forces of the proletariat and, in practice, harmony between labor and capital.

The trade unions, as economic organizations, breathe the same spirit; they embody the principle of binding the masses to the leader to be led by him out of hardship and misery into liberating socialism. The conception of socialism which corresponds to this spirit therefore also sees in the person of the leader the guarantee for the liberation of the working class. It can, if the working class acts in this spirit, lead in practice to nothing else than that the working class hands over all power to the leaders, sets them as masters over itself, and expects from them the fulfillment of its hopes and desires. The capable, faithful, non-traitorous leader thus becomes the core problem and ideal of the working-class movement. – *What a contrast there is between this ideology and revolutionary Marxism!*

Nowhere is it clearer than here that the Russian Bolsheviks are flesh from the flesh of the old Social Democracy. As leaders of the old type, they believe they can maneuver the proletariat and society into communism from their commanding height, and yet they are only the prisoners of their own system. Even if they think they are little Napoleons, they will not be able to cheat history, because the productive forces of society, once bound to a certain system, will follow the laws determined by it. The state of the leaders – as this dictatorship must be called – can only ever strive to increase its power and thus breeds itself its adversary, the exploited proletariat, until finally there is a revolutionary discharge, and a new order is born.

From the bottom up

If *Marx* sums up the task of the proletarian revolution as putting the means of production back into the hands of the producers expropriated by capital, state socialism is precisely opposed to this. The disposal of the means of production is taken from the workers and placed absolutely in the hands of the state. The state, however, which pompously proclaims itself to be the state of the workers and peasants, acquires as a centralized, state economic apparatus the character of domination over society, whose fullness of power dwarfs even the great capitalist trusts.

If the proletarian revolution is to lead to communism, it must bring the workers the actual disposal of the means of production, for only then is the proletariat able to determine its own destiny. In the KAPD and the General Workers' Union, for the first time in the history of the workers' movement, the way is being taken in practice to achieve the highest unity in the essence of the cause with the greatest independence and self-administration of the groups. What lives here in the first rudiments in the class-conscious proletariat must become the basic feature of the communist economy. Building on the self-administration of the operational units, the unifying bond around social production then wraps itself through their unification. The nature and content of the administration, however, is then – in contrast to state communism, where this is the task of the state and its leaders – a public matter. In the form of laws and guidelines – rules for the course of production and reproduction according to which the management of operational organizations must take place - the highest unity of the economy is achieved through self-management. It will be our task elsewhere to outline in detail the main features of this economic order. But without anticipating it, we can state with all certainty that the administration of the economy by the state trust never leads on the road to a classless society, but only means the reconstruction of the exploitative economy, albeit in a modified form.

Marx-Engels and Lenin: On the Role of the State in the Proletarian Revolution [17]

The economic revolution begins with the conquest of the means of production.

As soon as the rule of the working class has become a fact in an industrialized country, the proletariat is confronted with the task of carrying through the transformation of economic life on new foundations, those of communal labor. The abolition of private property is easily pronounced, it will be the first measure of the political rule of the working class. But that is only a juridical act that aims at providing the legal foundation for the real economic proceeding. The real transformation and the actual revolutionary work then only begins.

---

[17] This text originally appeared as a three part article in Proletarier, nrs. 4–6, *1927*. Its author Jan Appel signed with his pseudonym 'Max Hempel'. In*1932* a translation in Dutch language appeared as a pamphlet of the Group(s) of International Communists with the title 'Marxisme en staatscommunisme. Het afsterven van de staat' ("Marxism and State Communism. The Withering Away of the State"). The publication in Dutch was partly an adaptation. Original translation by F.K., 25-5-2016.
http://left-dis.nl/uk/GIC%20(1932)%20Marx-ism%20and%20state%20communism.1-0.pdf
The extensive footnotes documenting the differences in the 1927 and 1932 text versions have been omitted for this edition.

Leninist state communism.
The wage laborer remains a wage laborer.

To the extent that this problem is dealt with by the official Marxists, it is considered a foregone conclusion that the state has to accomplish this task. Since the 1917 revolution, the Russian Bolshevik Party has consistently implemented the idea of putting the means of production in the hands of the State. That this has only succeeded to a limited extent is due to the backward state of social production in Russia; in a sense, this is a natural barrier imposed upon the nationalization of the means of production. Therefore, the question is not whether and to what extent the nationalization is feasible, but rather whether the *nationalization of the means of production* by the victorious working class, as it manifests itself in Bolshevik theory and practice, is *the way leading to communism.*

To this question, the development of Russian enterprises under the Bolshevik government has given a clear answer. It has now become an established fact that the workers in the nationalized enterprises have remained *wage* laborers. The state has replaced the former private capitalists, and to this state, he sells his labor power. The state determines these wages by law and allows the union, which has become itself a state organ, to enact the labor laws. The wage laws actually in force in Russia show 17 wage classes, further piecework, bonuses, etc. In one word:

The nationalized industry is based on the exploitation of labor power like in the production under private capitalism.

The state bureaucracy becomes the ruling class.

In this system, Soviet elections are a sham.

The "free" workers finally conquer the "co-management" of the workers.

The state itself – which in Russia is called a workers' and peasants' state – as the owner of the means of production is *opposed* to the class of wage laborers. The centralized summit of the state bureaucracy is the legislative and executive organ of the state and, at the same time, the leader of the production. It occupies the same place as monopoly capital in private capitalism, and it represents in fact the new ruling class: the state bureaucracy and the peasant class. The workers sell their labor power to the state but can do so only according to the labor laws, in which the price and the working conditions are set by the state bureaucracy. Unprecedentedly harsh exploitation is prescribed by law and all opposition is in principle suppressed as counterrevolutionary. Discipline and subordination to the state complete this compulsory organization. One wonders in vain, in what way the first requirement of communism, "liberation from wage labor" has been accomplished.

On the other hand, to influence the economy and politics of the state, the workers, as well as the population

as a whole, are referred to Soviet elections and participation in the party and trade union life. However, as
the Soviet elections are decisively influenced by the al-
mighty state bureaucracy (and the propertied peasant
class), and as the party and the union are powerful instruments of bureaucracy, one will acknowledge that
the influence of the proletariat cannot come about in
this way. *Practically the latter is reduced to the "co-management" by the workers that the Social Democrats have demanded
under capitalism as well.*

"The association of free and equal producers"

According to Marx, the state is a special oppressive instrument – In capitalism: for the suppression of the
working class; Under the proletarian dictatorship: for
holding down the bourgeoisie and the counter-revolu-
tion.

However, it does not derive from this that in a communist society the state must become the exclusive
power in society through central leadership and the
concentration of the entire economic life in its hands.
Quite the contrary, both Marx and Engels have advocated the position that the hallmark of a communist
society lies in *"the association of free and equal producers"*
and that the state must disappear, when there is nothing left to suppress – thus when the resistance of the
bourgeoisie and its ideological influence over the workers have been overcome by them. "The association of
free and equal producers" does no longer know a class

antagonism and thereby in such a society the state as an instrument of power has become superfluous.

Lenin is the founder of *state communism*. Where he puts up the ground pillar for this theory in *"The State and Revolution"*, he refers to Marx and Engels. Although this work is written in defense of the proletarian dictatorship against Menshevism, and in this respect constitutes a lasting merit, the shape this dictatorship must take on according to Lenin is in contradiction to the conceptions on the issue of the founders of scientific communism. This can even be shown by the quotations that Lenin selects from the writings of Marx and Engels. Thus, Lenin quotes Engels:

> "The state, then, has not existed from all eternity. There have been societies that did without it, that had no idea of the state and state power. At a certain stage of economic development, which was necessarily bound up with the split of society into classes, the state became a necessity owing to this split. We are now rapidly approaching a stage in the development of production at which the existence of these classes not only will have ceased to be a necessity but will become a positive hindrance to production. They will fall as they arose at an earlier stage. Along with them, the state will inevitably fall. Society, which will reorganize production on the basis of a free and equal association of the producers, will put the whole machinery of state where it will then belong: into a

museum of antiquities, by the side of the spinning-wheel and the bronze axe." [18]

Engels says in another place, that the means of production will be state-owned. Therefore, Lenin founds his theory on this statement. But it must be a peculiar state, because it is only created (dictatorship of the proletariat), to give away, blow upon blow, all of its power, to gradually make itself superfluous. But what if the state concentrates in its hand "the administration of things and the leadership of production", and thereby secures its control over the workers even more by its management of the production system? If the administrative apparatus lies in the hands of a small party that also disposes of the political power, it is in reality about dominating the broad masses. Even the excuse that the party is "the party of the proletariat", does not change anything about this. One should always remember that this administrative apparatus, as the Russian example teaches, as *the central organizational apparatus*, can only be directed from the center. Within this apparatus, there is no place for "independent producers" (the workers). This would not correspond to the central leadership. As a consequence, we see that strict discipline, subordination to the commands of the top leadership,

---

[18] W. I. Lenin, "The State and Revolution" (Chapter I: Class Society and the State, Section 3. The State: an Instrument for the Exploitation of the Oppressed Class) https://www.marxists.org/archive/lenin/works/1917/staterev/ch01.htm#s4

has become a religious dogma of the Russian economy and politics.

The Soviet elections are supposed to provide – in theory – the safeguard that the state, who takes over the means of production "in the name of society", really manages the affairs, and directs the productive apparatus, in the name of society. Practice shows that the state bureaucracy enforces its plans with all means of power, and that soviet elections result in nothing. Thus, influencing state management by Soviet elections does not take place. This is neither the case in the State party (C.P.R.) nor in the union. The state bureaucracy does not permit the emergence of any other policies than its own. It does not need to be said that democracy in this state communism, namely by party and trade union organization and by Soviet elections, cannot provide a guarantee for the withering away of the state, which Marx and Engels demanded, and which Lenin imagined as well.

Production centralized in one hand defines a new form of domination. As a result, the state cannot wither away. Democracy cannot wither away either. Democracy remains the fig leaf to conceal oppression.

We conclude that this government or central leadership cannot wither away, but on the contrary has to affirm itself ever more, as a consequence of the way it took possession of the means of production. It actually means the subordination of the producers, who want to be free, to the government, their economic dependence on the latter, and thereby their subjugation. As a consolation, they then have the prospect to shape their own subjugation in accordance with their interests. However, this road is beyond their function as producers, it is the road of democracy.

Undoubtedly, as producers, the workers are a power, but as such, they must comply with the central leadership. Outside of the enterprises, they would only be a decisive power if they were armed. However, in Russia, we see that the workers have been disarmed and that, by contrast, a Red Army has been formed, which is at the disposition of the central government. As a result, in this democracy, the workers don't have the least impact. Essentially, it doesn't distinguish itself in any way from bourgeois democracy, and nothing can be done with it against a strong incumbent governing bureaucracy. (That this has become the case in Russia, first of all, depends upon the social relations in that country. These have secured victory for Russian state communism. But at the same time one can see from this what a blow it would be for the working class, should an effort be made to impose state communism according to the Russian model in highly developed capitalist countries).

The result of the state taking possession of the means of production according to the theory of Lenin, so the *central organizational leadership and management*, will be a new, strengthening state, namely an instrument of oppression by the ruling bureaucracy. Democracy will then be, as in bourgeois society, the fig leaf meant to cover the new domination over the workers.

Despite this, Lenin has expressed in *"The State and Revolution"* that this state must wither away, and he even comes to the correct conclusion that democracy must also die:

> "(...) in speaking of the state 'withering away', and the even more graphic and colorful 'dying down of itself', Engels refers quite clearly and definitely to the period after 'the state has taken possession of the means of production in the name of the whole of society', that is, after the socialist revolution. We all know that the political form of the 'state' at that time is the most complete democracy. But it never enters the head of any of the opportunists, who shamelessly distort Marxism, that Engels is consequently speaking here of democracy 'dying down of itself', or 'withering away'." [19]

Undoubtedly thereby Lenin meant democracy in state communism. Apart from the real development in Russia, which goes in the opposite direction, we are left to oppose by repeating the words of Engels:

> "The government of persons is replaced by the administration of things, and by the conduct of processes of

---

[19] W. I. Lenin, "The State and Revolution" (Chapter I: Class Society and the State, Section 4. The "Withering Away" of the State, and Violent Revolution.

production. The state is not 'abolished'. It withers away." [20]

It is clear that the theory of Lenin here is in contradiction with itself.

The contradiction in the Leninist theory of the state

Thus, it is necessary to expose the contradictions of the Leninist theory of the state. If the withering away of the proletarian state and its democracy are to be achieved, one cannot simultaneously force society politically and economically under the most stringent central leadership of the government. Because this is tantamount to the existence of a new state with greater power and wider competences than the bourgeois state has in capitalism. However, only political infants can believe that the state would release its power at a given time, even that it would be able to do so, without the collapse of the entire central apparatus build for production and administration. On the contrary, it will attempt to confirm its power and will grow into the biggest instrument for oppression society has ever seen.

A new ruling caste evolves in this new state communism. It consists of the leaders that rose from the working class and of defectors from the bourgeoisie,

---

[20] W. I. Lenin, "The State and Revolution" (Chapter I: Class Society and the State, Section 4. The "Withering Away" of the State, and Violent Revolution.

who put themselves into the service of state communism and who take over the central administration. This is what clearly comes to light in present-day Russia. Only a vanishing small part of the Russian workers was able to take a leading position in the administrative machinery of the nationalized production. To start up the economy, one needs to take over the functionaries and the leaders of the capitalist system. These people, legitimized as communists by their integration into the Communist Party, control the production of the country together with competent workers – the leaders. They constitute a new ruling caste and, already at present, use their position of power to take a much better material position than the workers. Touching complaints of Russian workers, that even penetrate official newspapers – such as the "Pravda" – (which is very telling in today's Russia) highlight that the bureaucrats only care for their own interests, without heeding the most glaring emergencies of the workers. It comes therefore as no surprise that the word *"Soviet bourgeoisie"* has arisen in Russia itself.

State communism stands in contradiction to the argument that in communism the state must wither away. Only either of two is possible: either state communism, i.e. central organizational leadership and management of production by the state – in that case, the state remains, and strengthens its power – or the withering away of the state and democracy, while society is going over to the association of free and equal producers, thereby rendering an oppressive state power superfluous. But in that case, the central apparatus for leading state production has to fall.

Lenin as a state communist

It is important to demonstrate that this new state repressive apparatus is not only born from the practice of Russian state capitalism but that Lenin has already sharply drawn its main lines in *"The State and Revolution"* (1917). He writes the following about it:

> "A witty German Social-Democrat of the seventies of the last century called the *postal service* an example of the socialist economic system. *This is very true.* At the present, the postal service is a business organized on the lines of state-*capitalist* monopoly. Imperialism is gradually transforming all trusts into organizations of a similar type, in which, standing over the "common" people, who are overworked and starved, one has the same bourgeois bureaucracy. But the mechanism of social management is here already to hand. Once we have overthrown the capitalists, crushed the resistance of these exploiters with the iron hand of the armed workers, and smashed the bureaucratic machinery of the modern state, we shall have a splendidly-equipped mechanism, freed from the "parasite", a mechanism which can very well be set going by the united workers themselves, who will hire technicians, foremen, and

accountants, and pay them *all*, as indeed *all* "state" officials in general, workmen's wages. Here is a concrete,
practical task which can immediately be fulfilled in relation to all trusts, a task whose fulfillment will rid the
working people of exploitation, a task which takes account of what the Commune had already begun to
practice (particularly in building up the state)."

"To organize *the whole* economy on the lines of the
postal service so that the technicians, foremen, and accountants, as well as all officials, shall receive salaries
no higher than "a workman's wage", all under the control and leadership of the armed proletariat – that is
our immediate aim. This is what will bring about the
abolition of parliamentarism and the preservation of
representative institutions. This is what will rid the la-
boring classes of the bourgeoisie's prostitution of
these institutions." [21]

Here Lenin plainly says that the central leadership and
management of the production in state communism will
be based on the model of the postal service, or rather,
effectuated in the manner of a state capitalist monopoly.
*"Technicians, foremen, and accountants, as well as all functionar-
ies"* are then state functionaries, functionaries in the state
production monopoly that controls the entire produc-

---

[21] W. I. Lenin, "The State and Revolution" (Chapter III: Experience
of the Paris Commune 1871, Section 3. Abolition of Parliamentarism

tion. *"A mechanism of general public enterprise, which is organized to the example of the capitalist state monopoly"*, [22] that indeed is the characteristic description for State Communism, as developed by Lenin.

It is necessary to point out here that Engels (and Marx in a different place) said: *"The proletariat seizes state power and turns the means of production into state property to begin with."* [23] It seems as if he says the same thing as Lenin, but he emphasizes, that the means of production *"first"* will be transferred into state ownership, and he further claims that taking possession of the means of production in the name of society, at the same time, constitutes the *"last independent act"* of the proletarian state.

This clearly shows that taking possession of the means of production just should initiate another act, which can only be – if we don't want to turn the teachings of Marx and Engels upside down – *"the association of free and equal producers"*. If taking possession of the means of production by the proletarian state initiates this association, then *"management of affairs"* and *"management of production processes"* will develop, while the associated society of free and equal producers arranges its life itself, on a free economic foundation. Only to the degree to which this association is extending itself, the oppressive force of the state becomes superfluous, the state can and will wither

---

[22] The GIC probably cites the Dutch translation of 'The State and Revolution' by Gorter.

[23] https://www.marxists.org/archive/marx/works/1877/anti-duhring/ch24.htm.

away. At the same time the calling into being of this association, which effectuates the withering away of the state, is the only task of the proletarian dictatorship. Only in this sense, we can understand the statement of Marx and Engels. Marx and Engels were careful not to present the taking into possession of the means of production by the state as a *"mechanism of the general public enterprise, organized to the example of the capitalist state monopoly."*

Such a view is merely the product of *"a witty social democrat"*, but it hasn't anything to do with Marx and Engels. Here Lenin has appropriated the way the *"witty social democrat"* explains Marxist doctrine, and necessarily took over the rigid, mechanistic conception of socialist society that shows itself in state communism. The state, which holds the monopoly of production, represents society here – in this respect, there is not the slightest difference with the social democratic theory of *nationalization.*

How Lenin solves the difficulty in a "simple" way

Lenin has been certainly aware that the concentration of the entire production in the hands of the State monopoly, which is based on the most stringent organizational centralism, means *a strengthening of state power.* However, when *"The State and Revolution"* was written, he could not in any way have foreseen the actual development in Russia. Here it was necessary – as the Bolsheviks wanted to remain in power – to strengthen state power as much as possible, that is, to establish a monopoly over production without regard to other purposes. Thereby the situation in Russia itself has developed Lenin's theory of State Communism. Step by step, the holders of Russian state power were prescribed the path to the fortification of the state. This process, which was started as a *"mechanism of the general public enterprise, organized to the example of the capitalist monopoly of the state"* had to become increasingly opposed to the *"free and equal producers"*.

Russia has developed the best example of Leninist state communism in reality, not as its bearers wished but as it had to develop.

Lenin could neither foresee all details of the actual outcome, but it was still clear to him that the proletarian state is a coercive institution as well. Moreover, he puts this in the foreground several times. Lenin now tries to solve the contradiction in an original way, how this state, that is still – according to the theory of Lenin – a permanent institute of central leadership and management of overall production will make itself redundant, will die down. In *"The State and Revolution"* Lenin proposes:

"We, the workers, shall organize large-scale production on the basis of what capitalism has already created, relying on our own experience as workers, establishing strict, iron discipline backed up by the state power of the armed workers. We shall reduce the role of state officials to that of simply carrying out our instructions as responsible, revocable, modestly paid "foremen and accountants" (of course, with the aid of technicians of all sorts, types and degrees). This is our proletarian task, this is what we can and must start with in accomplishing the proletarian revolution. Such a beginning, on the basis of large-scale production, will of itself lead to the gradual "withering away" of all bureaucracy, to the gradual creation of an order – an order without inverted commas, an order bearing no similarity to wage slavery – an order under which the functions of control and accounting, becoming more and more simple, will be performed by each in turn, will then become a habit and will finally die out as the special functions of a special section of the population." [24]

One recognizes clearly a mechanical organization to the extreme: in the economic field – as producers – the workers must adapt to the most severe discipline of state production monopoly and obey the state officials. These state officials are the "employers" who find their supreme leadership in the government. The workers have as well their supreme representation in government. Through political democracy (Soviet elections – party activity), they can influence the government and thereby control production with its state officials.

---

[24] W. I. Lenin, "The State and Revolution" (Chapter III: Experience of the Paris Commune 1871, Section 3. Abolition of Parliamentarism

We repeat that in such a system all power is concentrated in government, that the workers are more severely oppressed in this society than under capitalism, that democracy here is turned into a joke again, and that the prosperity of such society finally depends on the good will and capacities of the governmental men and their administration. Under such circumstances, the state *with* its democracy must give itself *firmer* foundations, rather than be redundant and die down, as Lenin wants as well. Lenin assures us that despite this the state will die, yes, that this would happen precisely because of this stringent organization. But he gives no argument for this but the quoted obscure reasoning that *"the functions of control and accounting, becoming more and more simple, will be performed by each in turn, will then become a habit and will finally die down as the special functions of a special section of the population."*

As already said, this is obscure, because if one can imagine this in general, then only in fantasy. To present the leadership of the state production monopoly ('postal service' or trust) as *functions of supervision and accounting that can be made very easy* is turning things on their head.

Therefore, we should stigmatize this argument of Lenin as a phrase without content, by which he disposed himself of conclusions that follow from the teachings of Marx and Engels about the withering away of the state – and that were troublesome for Lenin himself as well.

State communism clashes with the council idea

If one tries to follow the thoughts of state communism, one will soon find two peculiarities. First, state communism considers all problems only as mechanical ones. It sees everything solely from the point of view of how this and that area can be controlled *organizationally* and can be placed under central leadership and management.

That leads them to consider the carrying through of communism as the continuation of the concentration of business, as this already happens under capitalism. But what does the organization of production created by the concentration of capital mean? What does it mean, on the one hand, seen from the angle of the wage laborers and the position of the capitalists on the other?

It is the control of labor, the organized control of the wage laborers.

The Marxist analysis of capitalism does not leave the slightest doubt about it. For Marx, the social position of the capitalist as regarding the wage-laborer is characterized by his disposition over labor, over the workers in the production process.

The socialization theories of all currents of social democracy all concentrate on the same point of control over the working class. That labor must be dominated, is obvious for them and that this requires a strict central organization (because it is about a social, inseparably linked system), is likewise [considered] "natural".

But it is equally important that State Communism puts decisive weight on *the capacities of the leaders*. Very certainly this is a result of central organizational bundling because now everything depends on the ability and firmness of principle of the leaders placed in the center, to which the mass must subordinate in the strictest discipline.

One must admit to the Bolsheviks, that the working class only conquers power if it is a closed Unity, ready for struggle. However, whether this can be accomplished along the way of organizational discipline and subordination to a central command, is another question that will not be investigated now.

We draw attention to this phenomenon because it shows how state communism can be understood. *Decisive is that here all "leader"-problems are opposed to the council idea.*

A questionable departure from Marxism

The whole tactic of the workers' organizations that belong to the 3rd International - that is, which have state communism as their goal - is based on the idea of gathering large masses through the organization and directing them through central leaders. Once the organization has been created, the leader is the main thing. However, thereby the success of the proletarian revolution is highly conditioned upon the ability of leaders – a dubious deviation from Marxism.

This issue of leadership, which we encounter every day in the tactics of the parties and organizations of the 3rd

International (we only mention the trade union question, parliamentarism, and the organizational questions in the C.P. itself), has in state communism been transferred to the economic field as well. In this view, the ability and the attitude of the leader determine the fate of such a society to a large extent. Likewise, the glorification of Lenin and others, a sick worship of persons, can be explained.

"The emancipation of the workers must be the work of the workers themselves." These words do not lose their validity when considering the economic liberation of the workers. The most skilled leaders, even when the workers follow them in absolute discipline, cannot relieve the proletariat of its own liberating work. Moreover, if the proletarian dictatorship petrifies to the relationship of leader to mass, as expressed in State Communism, then this leadership develops, despite all democracy, into a new ruling caste, on which society becomes dependent.

The unified power of the workers is necessary.

When Russia, the country where a determined, heaven storming, revolutionary vanguard, who led a gloomy, dull mass of millions into revolution, has given birth to the doctrine of State Communism; when this doctrine, as the flaming fire signal of the first successful proletarian revolution, roused the enthusiasm of the workers in all countries, then its rigid bureaucracy, its re-established state power by the monopolizing of production, delivers the evidence that the final emancipation of the working class *cannot be brought about by state communism*, not by leaders to whom the mass is obedient by discipline, but only by the own strength of the workers themselves.

Of course, the united power of armed workers must crush the bourgeoisie, because only in this way the concentrated power of the bourgeois state can be vanquished. But here it is the workers themselves, armed based on the enterprises, who constitute the new state power.

The political unity of the workers' state, led by Councils or Soviets, whose head constitutes the Council Government, is *a necessary consequence of this struggle*. The abolition of private ownership of means of production and its declaration to "State" - or more accurately: social property, must also be carried out by the proletarian state, i.e. by the government.

The lessons of the Paris Commune (1871)

From here on, state communism branches off from Marxism, for it organizes state property under the central organizational direction of the government, removes the disposal of the means of production from the immediate producers, and places it in the hands of the government.

Marx and *Engels* however, demanded the transfer of the means of production into social property, social production by association, that is to say: *association of free and equal producers*. However, as we will demonstrate below, this is completely different from the central organization of production drawn to itself by the state.

In his *"Civil War in France,"* Marx has drawn lessons from the Paris Commune (1871), this first attempt to establish the power of the workers. Lenin in *"The State and Revolution"* serves himself with various quotations from it, to defend the dictatorship of the proletariat against the Social-Democrat Marx-falsifiers. We want to use the same quotations that Lenin utilized, to demonstrate that by "dictatorship of the proletariat" Marx meant something quite different from what it has become in Russia.

> "The first decree of the Commune, therefore, was the suppression of the standing army, and the substitution for it by the armed people."

> "The Commune was formed by the municipal councilors, chosen by universal suffrage in the various wards of the town, *responsible and revocable at any time.*"

> "The Commune," Marx wrote, "was to be a working, not a parliamentary, body, executive and legislative at the same time...."

> "Instead of deciding once in three or six years which member of the ruling class was to represent and repress [ver- and zertreten] the people in parliament, universal suffrage was to serve the people gathered in communes, as individual suffrage serves every other

employer in the search for workers, foremen, and accountants for his business. [25]

The council system according to Marx

Marx thus gave a striking characteristic of the proletarian council system, as it now has become a standard tenet of all revolutionary workers' parties. It must be well kept in mind that the Council appointed according to this exposition can be directly deposited by its voters at any time, just like employers appoint or dismiss workers, foremen, and accountants. The voters, the workers, are in this case complete masters of their "business"! How completely different the construction of the Commune was thought of, compared to central Russian State Communism, is shown by the following sentences from Marx:

"In a brief sketch of national organization, which the Commune had no time to develop, it states explicitly that the Commune was to be the political form of even the smallest village...." The communes were to elect the "National Delegation" in Paris.

"... The few but important functions which would still remain for a central government were not to be suppressed, as had been deliberately misstated, but were

---

[25] W. I. Lenin, "The State and Revolution" (Chapter III: Experience of the Paris Commune 1871, Section 3. Abolition of Parliamentarism

to be *transferred to communal, i.e., strictly responsible, officials."*

"... National unity was not to be broken, but, on the contrary, [was to be] organized by the communal constitution; it was to become a reality by the destruction of state power which posed as the embodiment of that unity yet wanted to be independent of, and superior to, the nation, on whose body it was but a parasitic excrescence. While the merely repressive organs of the old governmental power were to be amputated, its legitimate functions were to be wrested from an authority claiming the right to stand above society and *restored to the responsible servants of society."* [26]

The question of mass and leaders in the communes.

Unambiguously and clearly, it states here that the "few but important functions which would still remain for a central government" are to be exercised by communal officials who are strictly responsible at any moment to their immediate constituents. The executive officers of the Central Government are not *state* officials, but *communal* officials, not responsible to the government of the State, but to their direct voters in the Commune. Assuming the possibility of such an order (i.e. the central

---

[26] W. I. Lenin, "The State and Revolution" (Chapter III: Experience of the Paris Commune 1871, Section 4. Organization of National Unity

social functions are exercised by communal and therefore responsible officials of the Commune, which guarantee the unity of the country or society), also a withering away of the state can be imagined. But in such an order a state does no longer exist at all because what still can be called a central government has no separate power because it is in the hands of the Communes. The establishing of *the commune-* or *council system* in the whole country would thus be the simultaneous elimination of the parasitic State. "The merely repressive organs of the old governmental power were to be amputated, its legitimate functions were to be wrested from an authority claiming the right to stand above society and restored to the responsible servants of society". Once such an order has actually been carried through, the state has really died off, whereas society does not need it anymore.

The conditions for the withering away of the state

It's clear that this situation cannot exist under the dictatorship of the proletariat. Only when the former legitimate functions of state power, now to be called the central functions of society, can be transferred to the communal officials, a state power – here proletarian dictatorship – will be unnecessary. Whether these functions can be transferred depends on the commune exercising these central functions voluntarily and that these functions and measures to hold together society will find no resistance. The former state power must, as it were, come to life in the Communes, by creating a voluntary centralization for the exercise of the central functions and the monitoring of the resulting measures.

But because the main central functions of proletarian dictatorship consist of the abolition of private property and, furthermore, of all privileges, by transferring the means of production into social possession (by the association of free and equal producers), *all individuals that can lose these privileges or private property, or only their ideology,* will resist to these central functions. The functions of the new social order can therefore not be transferred to these persons or classes; as long as this resistance exists proletarian dictatorship is necessary. However, those Communes by which this resistance has been overcome, (for example when there is a large majority of workers who are loyal to Communism), could take over these functions themselves. Otherwise, the gradual withering away of the state is unthinkable.

But from this also follows that the proletarian state must be aware of depriving itself of all power from the beginning, by reassigning power into voluntary centralization, i.e. transferring it to the Communes. *To create these conditions is the <u>task</u> of the dictatorship, becoming superfluous is its <u>goal</u>.*

Opposition of the two systems

According to Marx, the few but important functions of the central government will be transferred to communal officials (strictly responsible to the Commune). Thus, when the local communal self-government has become a matter of course, the central state power is superfluous by voluntary centralization of Communes. *Lenin* agrees with this line of thinking and even makes it his own. However, according to the theory of *state communism* (also developed by Lenin), all means of production are state-owned, centralized in "the manner of a State Capitalist monopoly". This organizational *"mechanism of the general public enterprise"* presumes the leadership of the government. It is therefore an instrument of power of the State and not of the Communes.

And the functions of this monopoly, this organizational "mechanism of the general public enterprise", are exercised by officials that are responsible *to the central government and not to the communes.* A more glaring contrast than that which is reflected between the two systems is unthinkable.

Both views, however, Lenin thought to unite in his writing *"The State and Revolution"* and that this is possible, is the creed of all supporters of the 3rd International even today.

Economic foundations of communism [27]

In 1930, the Allgemeine Arbeiter Union (General Workers Union) published a study by Dutch council communists entitled: Fundamental Principles of Communist Production and Distribution. This analysis did not intend to propose any "plan" by which to arrive at a "better and more equal society." It deals exclusively with problems of the economy of communism and combines the practice of class struggle and social administration into an organic unity. The "Fundamental Principles", therefore, draw the economic consequences of a possible struggle conducted by the masses independently on the political level.

---

[27] Excerpt from: Henk Canne Meijer – Die Arbeiterrätebewegung in Deutschland (1918 -1938), Edition Soziale Revolution 1985.
https://www.anarchismus.at/ueber-den-tellerrand-blicken/raete-kommunismus/621-meijer-die-arbeiterraetebewegung-in-deutschland-1918-1933
Translation: Hermann Lueer.
Published in its original form in 1938 as a series of articles in the first four issues of the Marxist monthly periodical Radencommunisme, the text was completely revised in the 1950s and expanded to include, among other things, the part selected here. Translations of the last complete version are available in various languages, some of which differ slightly in scope and content. The selected excerpts are based on the German edition, but their content has been corrected in some places with reference to the English version - The Origins of the Movement for Workers' Councils in Germany.
https://www.marxists.org/subject/left-wing/gik/1938/workers-councils.htm

When the workers' councils will have conquered the rule, and when they will have learned by continuous effort to direct their struggles directly themselves, they will find themselves forced to give new foundations to their rule by consciously introducing new economic laws, in which the measure of working time will be the starting point of all production and distribution. The workers are capable of managing their production, but this is only possible if working time in the various industries is calculated on as broad a basis as possible and this measure is used in the distribution of goods.

The Fundamental Principles examine this problem from the standpoint of the exploited worker, who not only hopes that private property will be abolished but equally longs for the abolition of exploitation. But the history of our time has shown that the abolition of private property of the means of production does not necessarily entail the abolition of exploitation. One must analyze this question in more detail.

The anarchist movement grasped this necessity earlier than the Marxists, and its theoreticians paid strong attention to it. Nevertheless, their ideas have not been completely different from each other. If the Marxists, Social Democrats, and Bolshevists wanted to overcome the capitalist mode of production, which has reached the monopolistic stage, through a workers' state, without making fundamental changes in its mechanisms, the anarchists advocated a federation of free communes and rejected every form of state. This, however, was only to reconstruct it under other forms.

This point was the subject of intense controversy, we will give an example: one of the most famous anarchist theorists, Sebastian Faure, explained that the inhabitants of a commune measure the totality of their needs and productive capacities, then, after having surveyed the "total budget of needs of consumption and possibilities of production, region by region, the "National Committee" sets the norm and tells each region how much goods it can dispose of and what productive capacity it must provide. Equipped with this knowledge, each Regional Committee can do the same work for its region: set and make known to each communal committee what its commune has to dispose of and what it can provide. The last-named does the same with the members of the commune."[28]

To be sure, Sebastian Faure had previously determined in more detail that "each of these vast great organizations must have a voluntary agreement as to its basis and living principle," but an economic system requires economic principles, not well-intentioned, noble declarations. The same observation can be made based on a quotation from Hilferding, the famous theorist of social democracy, for here too the economic principle is missing: "The communal, regional and national commissars

---

[28] Sebastian Faure, My Communism (1921)

of socialist society decide how much and in what quantity and by what means new goods will be drawn from the natural or artificial conditions of production. With the help of production and consumption statistics, which capture the totality of social needs, they transform economic life as a whole according to the needs indicated in the statistics."[29]

The difference between these two principled positions can hardly be discerned. Nevertheless, the anarchists have the historical merit of having proclaimed the demand for the "abolition of the wage system." In this conception, however, the "National Committee," the "Bureau of Statistics," etc., what the Marxists call "people's government," is destined to pursue an economy in kind, i.e., an economy in which there is no longer any circulation of money. Housing, food, electricity, transportation, etc., are all "free." A certain number of goods and services remain payable in money (generally indexed upon the relationship between population and consumption). But despite these forms, the abolition of the wage does not mean the abolition of exploitation and even less does it mean social freedom. *And in fact, the more this sector of the economy in kind increases, the more the workers depend on the distributive apparatus for the determination of their "revenue".*

There was an example of an economy in kind where exchanges took place without money, at least for most of

---

[29] Rudolf Hilferding, Finance Capital (1920)

the goods, where housing, electricity, etc. were "free". This was the period of "war communism" in Russia. One could see not only that this system was not viable in the long run, but also that it could coexist without difficulty with a system built on class rule.

Consequently, reality has taught us: a) that it is possible to abolish private property without abolishing exploitation, and b) that it is possible to abolish wage labor without abolishing exploitation. If it is so, the problem of the Proletarian Revolution for the exploited arises in the following way:

– what are the economic conditions that allow the abolition of exploitation?

– what are the economic conditions that allow the proletariat to retain the political power once conquered and to tear out the economic roots of counterrevolution?

Although the "Fundamental Principles" examine the economic foundations of communism, their starting point is political rather than economic. It is not easy for the workers to conquer political-economic domination, but it is even more difficult for them to retain this domination. In the present conceptions of communism or socialism, there is a tendency – by facts, if not in words – to concentrate all the domination of social administration in some state or "social" offices. And conversely, this book ("Fundamental Principles") considers the economy as an inevitable continuation of the revolution and not as a desirable condition that will be realized in a hundred or a thousand years. It is a question of determining, based on the principles, the measures to be taken – not by a party or organization – but by the working class and its independent struggle organizations, the workers' councils. The realization of communism is not the business of a party, but the whole class, by determining in its councils and acting through its councils.

The producers and the social wealth

One of the great problems of the revolution is to establish new relations between the producer and social wealth, relations which under capitalist conditions are expressed through wage labor. The domination of wage labor is built on a deep contradiction between the value of labor power (wages) and the value of labor itself (the product of labor). For example, if the worker performs 50 hours of social labor, he receives as wages for it only, say, the equivalent of 10 hours. To truly emancipate himself, he must realize that it must no longer be the value of his labor-power that determines his wage, that determines his share in the mass of social products, but that this share must be determined by his labor itself. Labor as the measure of consumption is the principle to which he must give victory.

The difference between the sum of the labor performed and what the worker receives for it in exchange is called surplus labor and constitutes unpaid labor. The social wealth produced during this time represents the surplus product, and the value contained in this surplus product is called surplus value. Every society, whatever it may be, and consequently also the communist one, is based on the formation of surplus product because on the totality of the workers who perform useful or necessary work, some do not produce tangible goods. Their living conditions are consequently co-produced by the other workers (it is the same with health services, old people's homes, hospitals, administrative services, scientists, etc.). But it is *the way of producing* this surplus product, of distributing it, that constitutes capitalist exploitation. The worker receives a wage which, at best, is just enough to live reasonably under given conditions. He knows that he has given 50 hours of labor, but he does not know for how many hours he is paid with his wage (how many hours are included in his wage). He does not know the amount of his extra work. On the other hand, one knows how the ruling class consumes this surplus product: divided up, the social sectors receive a part of it, the factories need a part to enlarge their facilities, the administration, the police, and the army waste a large part.

In this discussion, we are particularly interested in two characters of the surplus product. First, that the working class has no or almost no say over the products of its unpaid labor, that it cannot estimate the value of its unpaid labor. Consequently, it cannot measure the importance of this extra work. It receives a wage, that is all; it has nothing to say in this distribution of social wealth. The class that has the means of production, the owning class, is the master of the production process and therefore of surplus labor. It makes the workers unemployed when it is in its interest, it uses the police against them or has them massacred in wars. The domination that the bourgeoisie exercises stems from the fact that it disposes of labor, of surplus labor, of surplus product. This condemns the proletariat to powerlessness in society and makes it an oppressed class. This analysis shows that oppression is equally strong whether it is exercised by private capitalism or by state capitalism.

One often hears it said that in Russia the exploitation of workers is abolished because private property is abolished and all the surplus product is at the disposal of the state, which distributes it in society by promulgating new social laws, building new factories, and developing production. To accept these arguments is to pass over the fact that the ruling class, the bureaucracy in charge of distributing the products, enriches itself through excessive wages, that it reproduces its positions of power by securing for its members the monopoly of higher education, and that the law of inheritance secures for it the accumulated wealth "for its family".

But even if we were to assume that this apparatus does not exploit the people. Then, as in Russia, the bureaucracy would remain the master of the labor process, that is, of surplus labor; it would dictate the conditions of work, with the help of the trade unions, among other things, just as can be seen in the Western countries. The function of the ruling bureaucracy is completely identical to that of the bourgeoisie, which directs private capitalism. If the bureaucracy does not exploit the people, it does not depend only on their good will to reject the opportunities offered to them. Then the development of society would no longer be a function of its economic and social necessities, it would depend on the "good" or "bad" will of its rulers. In other words, the relations of the workers to the wealth of society would, even in this case, be determined from outside, and the workers would have no means of influencing these relations, and there would be nothing left for them but to hope that "evil" leaders would become "good" ones.

In summary, this means that the abolition of the wage is not the *only and sufficient* condition for workers to receive the share of social wealth that they are entitled to, which they have created through their labor.

Certainly, this share can increase; but a *real abolition of the wage with all its forms* has a quite different character: without this real abolition, the working class cannot attain its power. A revolution that does not immediately abolish the wage relation must necessarily degenerate. The revolution thus "betrayed" leads to a totalitarian capitalist state.

One can also draw other conclusions. One of the essential tasks that fall to a group of workers who wish to radically eliminate capitalist exploitation – a revolutionary group, in other words, as it used to be called – is to give an economic foundation to the power conquered by political action. The time has passed when it was sufficient to demand only the abolition of capitalist private ownership of the means of production. It is also insufficient to demand only the abolition of wage labor. This demand in itself has no more consistency than a soap bubble if one does not know how to create the economic basis on which there is no more wage labor. A group that claims to be revolutionary and refuses to address this important question has no relevance to reality because it is incapable of proposing the image of a new world.

The "Fundamental Principles of Communist Production and Distribution" start from the following idea: all goods produced by human labor are considered qualitatively equal because they all contain a share of human labor. Only the different quantity of the labor they contain distinguishes them from one another. The measure of time by which the labor of each individual worker is calculated is the labor hour. This measure, intended to measure the quantity of labor which this or, that object contains, must be the social average labor hour. This is the measure that serves to determine the sum of wealth that society can dispose of, as well as the relations among the different sectors of the economy, and the part of social wealth that belongs to the worker. At this level, the "Fundamental Principles" develop an analysis and critique of the various theories – and also of the practices of the various currents that invoke Marxism, anarchism, or, more generally, socialism. One finds in it a more detailed exposition of the brief principles left by Marx and Engels in Capital, the Critique of the Gotha Program, and the Anti-Dühring.

Well understood, the "Fundamental Principles" do not limit themselves to studying the unit of calculation of communism; they also analyze its applicability in production and the distribution of the social product and the "public services", reviewing the new rules of social accounting, the extension of production under the control of the workers, the disappearance of the market, etc., and finally the applicability of communism to agriculture through the intermediary of peasant cooperatives, which also calculate their harvests in units of labor time.

Thus, the "Fundamental Principles" have as their starting point the empirical fact that, at the time of the proletariat's assumption of power, the means of production are in the hands of the business organizations. It depends on the communist consciousness of the proletariat, which arises in the struggle itself, the subsequent fate of these means of production, the fact of whether the proletariat will keep them in hands or not. The main problem that the proletarian revolution will have to solve will be to determine the invariable relations between the producers and the social product, and this can only be done by introducing the labor-time calculation into production and distribution. This is the most far-reaching demand that the proletariat could make, but at the same time, it is the minimum of what it must demand. And consequently, a question of domination that can be solved by the proletariat alone, without the help of any other social group. ... This is also the only type of domination that the implementation of the working time calculation requires. *This is the last message that the revolutionary movements of the 1st half of the XX century have left us.*

Literature and Sources

Henk Canne Meijer
>	Die Arbeiterrätebewegung in Deutschland (1918
>	- 1933) (The Workers' Council Movement in
>	Germany). Edition Soziale Revolution, 1985.
>	Translation: Hermann Lueer.
>
>	Alternative English translation under the title:
>	The Origins of the Movement for Workers'
>	Councils in Germany.
>	https://www.marxists.org/subject/left-
>	wing/gik/1938/workers-councils.htm

Frederick Engels
>	Anti-Dühring, 1877
>	https://www.marxists.org/ar-
>	chive/marx/works/1877/anti-
>	duhring/ch26.htm

Frederick Engels
>	Socialism: Utopian and Scientific
>	https://www.marxists.org/ar-
>	chive/marx/works/1880/soc-utop/ch03.htm

Frederick Engels
>	Origin of the Family, Private Property, and the
>	State
>	https://www.marxists.org/ar-
>	chive/marx/works/down-
>	load/pdf/origin_family.pdf;

Group of International Communists
        Fundamental Principles of Communist Produc-
        tion and Distribution, Red & Black Books 2020

Group of International Communists
        Internationale Rätekorrespondenz 1934 - 1937
        (International Council Correspondence) Theo-
        retical and Discussion Organ for the Councils
        Movement. Issue of the Group of International
        Communists - Holland.
        The selected articles were also published in: In-
        ternational Council Correspondence, Chicago,
        Illinois, U.S.A.,
        http://www.aaap.be/Pdf/International-Coun-
        cil-Correspondence/International-Council-Cor-
        respondence-2-12a.pdf
        https://www.marxists.org/subject/left-
        wing/icc/index.htm

Max Hempel (pseudonym of Jan Appel)
        Das russische Wiederaufbauprogramm (The
        Russian Reconstruction Program), from: Prole-
        tarier, *1926*, Vol. 10, p. 175.

Max Hempel (pseudonym of Jan Appel)
        Marx-Engels und Lenin. Über die Rolle des
        Staates in der proletarischen Revolution (Marx-
        Engels and Lenin: On the Role of the State in
        the Proletarian Revolution).
        from: *Proletarier, 1927*. In1932 a translation in
        Dutch language appeared as a pamphlet of the
        Group(s) of International Communists with the
        title 'Marxisme en staatscommunisme. Het af-

sterven van de staat' ("Marxism and State Communism. The Withering Away of the State").
The publication in Dutch was partly an adaptation.
Original translation by F.K., 25-5-2016.
http://left-dis.nl/uk/GIC%20(1932)%20Marxism%20and%20state%20communism.1-0.pdf

W. I. Lenin,
The State and Revolution
https://www.marxists.org/archive/lenin/works/1917/staterev/ch01.htm

Karl Marx
Critique of the Gotha Programme
https://www.marxists.org/archive/marx/works/1875/gotha/ch01.htm

Karl Marx
Capital. A Critique of Political Economy, Volume I
https://www.marxists.org/archive/marx/works/download/pdf/Capital-Volume-I.pdf

Group of International Communists

FUNDAMENTAL PRINCIPLES OF COMMUNIST PRODUCTION AND DISTRIBUTION

"As simple as the basis for the domination of the working class is, as simple is the *formulation* for the abolition of wage slavery (even if the practical implementation is not so simple!). This abolition can only consist in the abolition of the separation of work and the work product, that the *right of disposal* over the work product and therefore also over the means of production is again given to the workers."

RED & BLACK BOOKS

The *"Fundamental Principles of Communist Production and Distribution"* emerged as a reaction to the negative development of the Russian Revolution. With this writing, the authors, for the first time, put up for debate the *economic foundations* for the construction and organization of a society in the sense of the *"association of free and equal people"*. At the same time, they took into account all the experience gained from the previous attempts of the labor movement, and by criticizing it were able to point out necessary new paths. A critique that has lost nothing of its original topicality to this day.

The first edition of the Fundamental Principles, published in German in 1930, was confiscated and largely destroyed. A completely revised and improved edition in Dutch was first published in excerpts in 1931 and 1935 in book form in a second edition. The text of the German first edition was reprinted in 1970 and also translated into English and French. The completely revised and improved 2nd edition, on the other hand, remained largely unnoticed in Dutch for the following 85 years. With this translation of the 2nd edition into English, the Sleeping Beauty has awakened.

HERMANN LUEER **FUNDAMENTAL PRINCIPLES OF COMMUNIST PRODUCTION AND DISTRIBUTION**

RED & BLACK BOOKS

This book is a tribute to the collective work of the Group of International Communists of Holland. Given the experiences with state communism in Russia, their "Fundamental Principles of Communist Production and Distribution," published in 1930, was an attempt to elaborate the economic basis of a communist society as outlined by Karl Marx and Friedrich Engels. Although their explanations have lost none of their original topicality, their text has remained a product of its time in the way they address the literature of that period. This paper, therefore, attempts to reintroduce the core statements of the "Fundamental Principles of Communist Production and Distribution" into the current debate on alternatives to capitalism.

CRITIQUE OF CAPITALISM

AND THE QUESTION OF THE ALTERNATIVE

RED & BLACK BOOKS

Mistakes in the explanation of the cause of a disturbing effect usually continue in a wrong proposal for a solution. Those who explain poverty as the result of market failure look for alternatives to market regulation. Those who explain poverty as a necessary consequence of the market-based production relationship want to abolish the market. Any alternative to capitalism is therefore only as good as the underlying explanation of the capitalist mode of production to which it is supposed to be an alternative. Accordingly, the present book is not about imagining a better world, regardless of the reasons for the worldwide impoverishment and misery of large parts of the population, but about deriving from the explanation of capitalism the basic principles of an economy beyond capitalism. Critique and alternative are thus brought together. The question of feasibility is thereby resolved by itself.

HERMANN
LUEER
Great Depression 2.0
ARGUMENTS
AGAINST
CAPITALISM

RED & BLACK BOOKS

Government rescue programs for bad loans are designed to prevent a credit crunch.

Worldwide debt is rising to many times the annual economic output.

To stabilize the global financial system, central banks are buying government and corporate bonds on an ever-increasing scale.

Negative interest rates are intended to revive the economy.

"Helicopter Money" - the printing and distribution of money are being discussed as a solution.

Is the capitalist financial system on the verge of collapse?

Are we experiencing a new Great Depression?

What exactly is a Great Depression?

Why can too much wealth in the form of overcapacity become the cause of mass impoverishment?

HERMANN LUEER

WHY HUNGER?

ARGUMENTS
AGAINST
THE MARKET

RED & BLACK BOOKS

Despite the wonders of technology in the 21st century, global hunger, no access to clean water, bitter poverty, and miserable working conditions accompany the globalized market economy. Not only in the so-called developing countries, but in the successful industrial nations as well, the official poverty reports point up the growing discrepancy between what is presented as the wealth of the nation in the gross national product and calculated as per capita income and that what the majority of the population gets from this.

The question of the alternative to these achievements of the global market economy begins with arguments against the market. The classic of this critical analysis – »Capital« by Karl Marx – thus inevitably enjoys a renaissance. The guy got it right!

9 783982 206578